# THE MAGIC BEHIND NUMBERS

### SHIVAM SINHA

Copyright © Shivam Sinha
All Rights Reserved.

<u>Dedicated to my parents, teachers, friends
and to my hardwork and dedication</u>

# Contents


*Acknowledgements*     *vii*

*Preface*     *ix*

**Volume 1 : The Beginning Of A Big Theory**

1. Infinity And Mathematics     3

2. The History Of Numbers     6

3. The Technique Involved     9

4. Infinity And The Paradox     11

5. The First Step     14

6. The Key Factors     16

7. The Shocking Discovery     18

8. The Theory Of Conflicting Equations     23

9. The Conclusion     27

10. The Paradox     29

11. About The Future     31

12. About The Author     33

13. About The Book     36

# ACKNOWLEDGEMENTS

I take this moment to thank my parents who have always been the best guide for me. They would guide me through my problems and always try to motivate me in one way or another. They made sure I went on to the right path and took right decisions. If it were not for them, I won't be in the position I am in now and writing a book by myself would still be a fantasy to this day.

I also thank my friends who have in some way or other helped me in this theory. After I came up with the discovery they would try to help and figure out something more to it. They have given me tons of idea and interesting theories on which I am working to this day.

I also thank my teachers who helped me during the times I faced any academic related problem. They would always be willing to help me in any circumstance.

In the end, I would like to thank myself for working hard on this theory and not giving up until the end. There were times when I thought that this theory was a waste and in the end was of no use, but I never gave up and finally finished a masterpiece theory.

# PREFACE

I have always wondered about how maths first began or how do numbers actually work. Desperate to find an answer for the same, I would spend hours scribbling random formulae on my notebook to try and make something out of it. Until one day, I was looking through some random algebra problems when I saw this problem appear -:

$$\sqrt{2 + \sqrt{2 + \sqrt{2 + \cdots}}}$$

An infinite radical sum - Source : Wikipedia

Now the curious me, who had never seen such a problem started to solve it immediately, but here comes the turning point - what I really saw at that time was :

$\sqrt{2} + \sqrt{2} + \sqrt{2} + \sqrt{2} \ldots$

Now, we know that if a number is added 'x' number of times, it basically means multiplying the number by 'x'. But in this case, as the number of terms was infinite the value for this problem would eventually lead to infinity.

This was the first time I was shocked at how such an easy problem cannot be solved. The questions were roaming around my mind - "Why do we have something such as infinity?... Isn't infinity just another word for 'no solution' in this question?"

That is why I felt a sudden urge to find a solution to this problem and go in-depth into the problem. After giving the question numerous attempts I stumbled upon a rather interesting but wierd theory. This book includes my thoughts during the process and how I actually came up with the theory. I hope you find this book Informative and interesting.

# Volume 1 : The beginning of a big theory

# I

# Infinity and Mathematics

Before I start my point of view on Infinity, I would like to debunk some myths about the term "Infinity".

- First of all, Infinity is **not** a number. It is something which is out of the limits of a number.
- Then, the size of inifinity is something which cannot be determined using the current technology we have.
- Infinity is not something which is present as a number. Rather, it is a theory which we have come up with to help solve some problems and equations.

Now for example, take the series : "1+2+3+4+5+6+7+8 . . . +∞" which is also commonly known as "Ramanujan's Summation". It currently has a debate going around where Srinivas Ramanujan Sir stated that this summation is equal to -1/12 which is roughly equal to -0.083. Surprising isn't it? He was able to find a solution which is basically impossible.

His method of solving was simple and understandable, although we won't be going much deep into that. But, after this summation was solved, we were able to pinpoint one of the major loopholes of Mathematics : **"Infinity"**.

His way of solving the summation was as follows :

- Let A = 1-1+1-1+1-1+1-1+1-1. . .
- 1-A = 1-(1-1+1-1+1-1+1-1+1-1. . .) : Opening the bracket we get--
- 1-A = 1-1+1-1+1-1+1-1. . . which is saying the same as--
- 1-A= A
- And we get A = 1/2

Now for the second step :
- Let B = 1-2+3-4+5-6+7-8. . .
- A-B = (1-1+1-1+1-1+1-1. .) - (1-2+3-4+5-6+7-8. .)
- Regrouping the terms we get :
- A-B = (1-1)+(-1+2)+(1-3)+(-1+4). . .
- A-B = 1-2+3-4+5-6. . .
- A-B = B
- A = 2B
- B = A/2 (A=1/2)
- B = 1/4

For the final step :
- Let S = 1+2+3+4+5+6+7+8. . . $\infty$
- B-S = (1-2+3-4+5-6+7. . .) - (1+2+3+4+5+6+7. . .)
- B-S = (1-1) + (-2-2) + (3-3) + (-4-4) . . .
- B-S = -4-8-12-16-20. . .
- B-S = -4(1+2+3+4+5+6. . .)
- B-S = -4S
- B = -3S

- $S = -B/3$ ($B = 1/4$)
- **$S = -1/12$**

It is almost unimaginable how something like this could even happen. Because as we keep adding the numbers, the sum keeps getting bigger and bigger. But, according to this summation the answer came in negative?! This presents to us the loopholes in Mathematics and shows us how Mathematics still has a long way to go.

My theory also relates to the above theory but instead of proving that the sum of all numbers is negative, I have managed to prove something which rather seems even more impossible.

In the next section I'll be telling you about the methods I used to reach my theory. I'll be explaining each and every method in detail so that it will be reader-friendly to all the readers.

# II
## The History of Numbers

Now, before going on right to the theory, first let us have a look at the history of numbers. The first solid evidence of the existence of the number **one**, and that someone was using it to count, appears about 20,000 years ago. It was just a unified series of unified lines cut into a bone. It's called the Ishango Bone.

Now, many others say that counting first began in Sumeria in 4000 BC. It was considered as one of the oldest civilizations and is also mostly given the credit for the discovery of numbers.

But, if you look at it another way, during the times when the human race started, especially the cavemen times, when people starting livng in groups, there can be a major possibility that numbers were there at that time too. For example, take the ice age, which lasted until 11,000 years ago. During that time, when people would hunt for food and store food how do you think they kept a stock on how much food do they have, or have many weapons do they have, or even how many people are in the group? Of course, they did not use modern day number systems, but they surely had a way of counting. Most of the theories and proofs say that people in those times used something similar to tally marks to count. The number of strokes used to represent the number of items of that category etc.

By now, our generation is far more advanced in Maths having a lot of complex theories and a lot of different formulae. But, even after advancing so much in Maths, we still have a lot of problems unsolved.
For example, we have the Millenium problems, in which there are problems which have not been able to be solved even after 200-300 years. We have the famous Riemann Hypothesis, which presents complex analysis in maths and a lot of complex number theory.

But, one of the most common, but still one of the most problematic theories in the existence of Mathematics is the term Infinity. Infinity is something which we all believe is "**never ending**". But, there is more to it than we think. Infinity cannot be concluded in a simple two word term like 'never ending'. It is something which is rather more complex and pretty much unsolved.

'Why do we have something as Infinity?', comes to the mind of many people when they first hear about it. Isn't infinity just a way of telling us that a problem has no solution? Or is infinity something which still needs to be decoded. It is as if infinity is a code which hides a lot of secrets to mathematics. If the term **Infinity** is decoded we would be able to solve many more complex theories and Maths would be way more advanced than it is now.

Overall speaking about infinity gives you an idea of how much Maths is still missing out. Believe it or not, most of the things run around Maths. That is why Maths is phrased as the "Language of the universe".
Maybe, reading this must have got you curious about Infinity. I was curious at first too, and using the theory I have discovered I feel like it is going to give you an idea of how infinity actually works and how far under developed Maths actually is right now.

In the next section, I'll be giving you a brief idea of my theory and how I connect it to Infinity. The theory is so vast that it gives openings to other theories and other possibilites in the field of Maths. I am taking this oppurtunity to present to you my thoughts on the current Maths and the loopholes present in it which need to be solved.

# III

# The Technique Involved

This section focuses on the technique which is most used in the whole derivation of the theory : "**Regrouping**". This technique is a commonly ignored technique although it has great importance in a lot of problems. Let us have a look at what this technique really states :

Consider the problem -: (2+3+7+6) - (2+3+6+4)

Now one way you can solve this problem is by adding the numbers and then simplifying eventually leading to 18 - 15 = 3.

But, what if the number of terms in each bracket was a lot, lets say a 1000 terms. In cases like these, regrouping is the more efficient method.

What I am gonna do here is take the first term of each bracket, that is 2 and 2, but note that there is a negative sign outside the $2^{nd}$ bracket, so we take the second 2 as (-2).

Now, the next step we do is combine them together and write them as (2+(-2)) or simply (2-2).
After this repeat the procedure with the second, third and fourth terms of each brack and you get :
(3-3), (7-6), (6-4).

Now, as we have already taken the negative sign into consideration we can just add all these combinations together to get : (2-2)+(3-3)+(7-6)+(6-4) which simplifies to 1+2 = 3.

This can be represented mathematically as follows :

$$(a+b+c+d+e+f) - (g+h+i+j+k+l) = (a-g)+(b-h)+(c-i)+(d-j)+(e-k)+(f-l).$$

If you read the previous chapter, you will notice that this technique was also used by Ramanujan, to derive and solve the summation : (1+2+3+4+5+6+7+8+9. . . ∞).

Keep in mind that this the only technique which will be used in the whole derivation and you can already start to make out that the derivation is not all that complicated.

In the next section, I'll be telling you more about Infinity and the relation between the Ramanujan Summation. I will also be listing out the counter arguments for the Ramanujan Summation and why it isn't stated as a complete success.

# IV

## Infinity and the Paradox

Now that you have been accquainted with the information about the Ramanujan Summation let us rethink over the term 'Infinity'.

Till now, we would believe that something like 1+2+3+4+5+6+7+8+9...∞ would obviously lead to infinity.
I mean think about it as you keep adding the numbers the value of the sum keeps increasing and it starts to approach what we assume as infinity.

To give you an idea of what I am saying, take a look at the graph below :

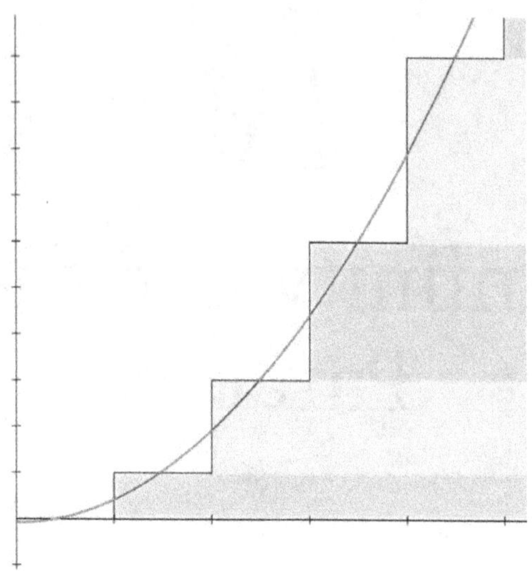

The Ramanujan Summation Graphed - Source :
Wikipedia

As you can see, the curve in the graph represents the equation $Y = 1+2+3+4+5\ldots\infty$. You can observe that the curve first starts to gradually curve upwards but later the curve starts to steep rapidly. You can also observe that once it has curved upwards it does not curve downwards and that its value approaches towards Infinity.

But then, the summation presented by Ramanujan Sir achieved a result completely different from the expected result. So, the question arised or rather a debate arisedon which solution was actually correct.

Ramanujan's solution did not seem to have any fault logically, but the result was not something which could be believed. On the other hand the other solution didn't exactly have a proper derivation or a proper proof.

After this fierce debate continued, another solution suddenly arised for this very problem. Let me give you a quick run-through of the solution.

Let $S = 1+2+3+4+5+6+7+8+9\ldots\infty$

Now grouping the terms specifically we get :

- $S = 1 + (2+3+4) + (5+6+7) + (8+9+10) + (11+12+13)\ldots\infty$
- From here $S = 1+9+18+27+36+45+54\ldots\infty$
- Taking out 9 common from the terms we get :
- $S = 1+9(1+2+3+4+5+6+7+8\ldots\infty)$
- $S = 1+9S$
- $-8S = 1$
- **$S = -1/8$**

Now, this was another big shock for everyone as this was also an unexpected solution. Now we have not one, but 2 negative solutions : -0.084 and -0.125. This was something very wild and no one had expected such an outcome. In the end no one has been able to conclude anything yet as the range of the answers is rather bizzare. Hence, the mystery of infinity still remains. .

In the next section I will be explaining on how I was able to derive a theory by mistake!

# V
# The First Step

gSo, my story goes as follows :

I have loved doing maths as a kid. I would love to try challenging problems and try to come up with an answer to each of them. By the time I was in $9^{th}$, I already started studying for higher classes, but I felt as if the process was incomplete. When I was in $9^{th}$, I found out that a friend of mine had discovered a formula in the field of Physics. I was completely amazed at how a 14 year old is able to discover such a formula. Motivated by him, I started working on my own formula, but I didn't know where to start. After all, creating a formula or discovering a formula is not an easy task, is it? You have to spend days looking through theories and formulas and try to combine some of them and maybe you could be the one who ends up creating another formula. So, that was when my journey towards the creation of my theory started.

Now, I'll tell you a bit on how I actually discovered the theory. As usual I spent my days reading up on interesting theories and solving questions related to my syllabus. That was how my normal day was, but then, one day when I was practicing some problems I came up to this problem.

$$\sqrt{2 + \sqrt{2 + \sqrt{2 + \cdots}}}$$

An infinite radical sum - Source : Wikipedia

Now this is a pretty normal question which could be easily solved by substitution and squaring, but when I had the first look on this question I seemed pretty confused. That was because I read the question as :

$\sqrt{2} + \sqrt{2} + \sqrt{2} + \sqrt{2} \ldots$ up until infinity terms
Now this was just a mistake of the eye and I immediately said that the answer was Infinity, but I don't know why I had a feeling that this question was something more deep. Immediately, I started solving it and trying different methods and different formulae, I know it is wierd but I had a strong feeling that it was connected to something more deep.

This was when I had gotten the first few hints for my theory. So, yes my first theory was actually created by mistake! Coming up in the next section I am going to be naming the key factors responsible for my theory, whether that be the series which I used or the techniques I used.

# VI

# The Key Factors

To come up with this theory, I did not need a lot of things to start with. Let me list out the important series which were used to come up with this theory, while briefly explaining each.

- The first series, which is also the most important series in the theory is :
  **1+1+1+1+1+1+1+1+1+1+1+1+1+1+1+1.** . . which can also be described as the following :
- 1) An infinite AP with common difference = 0
- 2) An infinite GP with common ratio = 1

If we were to try and solve this series using the infinite GP formula : a/1-r (where a=1 and r=1) we would end up with 1/0 which basically means - tending towards infinity.

This series is of utmost importance as most of the theory is based around this series.

- The second series is one which we have already discussed about and is a pretty famous series that is :

- 1+2+3+4+5+6. . . which is also the Ramanujan Summation or as the sum of all natural numbers.

This series is also very important as we are going to be combing it with the first series to give the theory the important base it needs.

This is pretty much all we need in the derivation of the theory, along with the method '**Regrouping**' which I have already talked about earlier.

Coming up next, is going to be the long awaited derivation and disclosure of the theory which I have discovered.

# VII

## The Shocking Discovery

To begin with the disclosure of the theory, let me present you with a mind-boggling discovery.

Let us first start off with the series : 1+1+1+1+1+1+1+1...

- Let A = 1+1+1+1+1+1+1...
- Now 1+A = 1+(1+1+1+1+1+1+1+1...)
- 1+A = 1+1+1+1+1. . . (The number of terms on RHS will not change as the number of original terms was already infinite)
- 1+A = A
- 1 = A-A
- **1 = 0**

Seems impossible right? Then how was I able to derive such a solution using simple mathematics? This might give you an idea of how interesting maths can be. **The equation**

**1=0 already sounds and seems impossible** but using just simple maths I was easily able to come to this solution.

Now let us analyze what we have seen here :

- First of all, we had a series which already looked like it would sum up to infinity.
- Now as you keep adding the terms you would see that the number keeps getting larger by each term.
- But, when we regroup the equation and do some changes to it, we suddenly end up with the equation **1=0**.
- Not only is the solution not infinity, it is even smaller than any of the terms of the series (0<1).

To conclude, we have been able to analyze that the equation 1+1+1+1... when changed a bit derives to a final equation of 1=0.

But, if you think that this is the theory here, then you have been mistaken, because there is a whole lot more to this theory.

For now, let us note the fact that we have derived the equation 1=0. (Result 1)

Now let us move on to the $2^{nd}$ result/derivation.

## The Second Result

This second result can be somewhat related to the first one so read it carefully as we would be making some deductions from the result.

- Let B = 1-1-1-1-1-1-1-1-1-1 . . .
- 1-B = 1-(1-1-1-1-1-1-1-1-1-1 . . .)
- 1-B = 1-1+1+1+1+1+1+1. . .
- 1-B = A

- $A + B = 1$

Now as you can see this result seems farely normal as after simplying the calculation all the 1s and -1s will be striked off and we would only be left with a single 1 from the series B.

Let us keep this fact in mind and conclude that A+B=1 (Result 2)

## The Third Result

The next result is going to be of great importance as it is going to be the one which you could say adds spice to the theory. Let's have a look at it :

Let A = 1+1+1+1+1+1+1+1...

Let B = 1-1-1-1-1-1-1-1-1...

- A-B = (1+1+1+1+1+1...) - (1-1-1-1-1-1...)
- A-B = 1+1+1+1+1+1... -1+1+1+1+1+1+1+1...
- A-B = 1+1+1+1+1+1+1+1...
- A-B = A
- A-A = B
- B = 0

Can you even believe what you are seeing here? When I had first derived this I had to recheck again and again to see if I made any errors. But as it seems, there were no errors in the calculation.

From the following result. we can conclude that :

- We had a series B = 1-1-1-1-1-1-1-1...
- As it may seems the value of the series must tend to negative infinity.

- But after combing it with series A we were able to make some deductions and arrive at the result that the series B has converged to 0.

This infact is something very important in the upcoming procedure are I am going to be deriving some even more important results which will be surprising you even more.

So, here we were able to conclude, that the series B : 1-1-1-1-1-1-1-1... converges to 0. (Result 3)

But, let's go back to Result 2. We were able to derive that the value of the equation A+B = 1.

Here we were able to derive that B=0, so substituting the value of B=0 in Result 2 we get :

- A+0 = 1
- A = 1

Here, we have something even more fantastic; after proving that the series B : 1-1-1-1-1-1... = 0, we are now able to do some deductions and arrive at our $4^{th}$ result which states that : 1+1+1+1+1+1+1... = 1

So, concluding all our results we have arrived at some amazing but unbelievable results.

Let me summarize the results which we were able to conclude from the above results :

- **Equation 1 -: The series - 1+1+1+1+1+1+1+1... converges to 1**
- **Equation 2 -: The series - 1-1-1-1-1-1-1-1-1... converges to 0**
- **Equation 3 -: We were able to simplify result 1 and end up with 1 = 0**

Keep in the mind that we will be giving more importance to the third result as it is going to be extremely important later.

# VIII

## The Theory of Conflicting Equations

By now, we have had a look on some pretty interesting and deep theories. But this is just the beginning of my main theory.

After having a look at the current results, we can say that Maths definitely has a lot of loopholes and they are something which should be solved. We don't know how these theories could be useful in the future so we should atleast be willing to discover more about them.

Now for my next result, which also defines the theory, I would like the reader to note that this theory is related to all the results we have previously derived, whether it be directly or indirectly.

## The Main Result

Let us start with 3 series :

- Let A = 1+1+1+1+1+1+1 . . .
- Let B = 1-1-1-1-1-1-1-1-1 . . .
- Let C = 1+2+3+4+5+6+7+8 . . .

As you can already see we are starting off with the 3 common series which we have been using the entire time. Just by playing with these series, we are able to pull off some great results.

Now, let us start the derivation. Kindly pay attention to the method used. It is going to be pretty easy to understand as it will be using the same techniques as used in the previous derivations.

- C-A = (1+2+3+4+5. . .) - (1+1+1+1+1. . .)
- C-A = (1-1)+(2-1)+(3-1)+(4-1) . . .

Now, as you can see we are finally making use of the regrouping method which was explained in Chapter 3.

- C-A = 0+1+2+3+4+5+6 . . .
- C-A = C
- C-C = A
- **A = 0** (Result 5)

Notice something odd here? In the previous chapter we derived the value for A to be 1, but here we are arriving with A to be 0?

Equating (Result 5) with (Result 4) we get :

A = 0 and A = 1

So to conclude A = 0 = 1 or simply 1 = 0

Looking at this, are you able to recall something? In the previous chapter Result 1, we were able to derive the same result that is 1 = 0.

Now, this is the main theory here. As you can see, we have 2 results A = 0 and A = 1 which would in turn give B = 1 and B = 0 (A+B=1 : Result 2)

We are having 2 conflicting theories that is 2 conflicting equations, but if we look at it closely, in the end all the theories were able to conclude at 1 point - (1 = 0).

Something which was the most unbelievable at first is now being proved by all equations directly.

To conclude, **from the Theory of Conflicting Equations we are able to arrive at the equation 1 = 0.**

Now, why did I spend all this time proving such a simple equation? Well, let me give you some insight on the equation's meaning.

- Let us start with the equation 1 = 0
- Rearrange the equation to 0 = 1
- Add 1 to both sides.
- 0+1 = 1+1
- 1 = 2
- Keep repeating the same procedure. You will see that something even more complicated has been proved.
- Let the number on LHS be 'n'
- Then, the number on RHS would automatically be 'n+1'.
- Equating them both, we get : **'n = n+1'**

To give you an idea on why this equation is so important, during all these years the equation n = n+1 has been termed mathematically impossible. But, after my derivations I was able to prove the existence of the equation n = n+1.

This is honestly one of the biggest proofs in mathematics till date. This proof is something which has the capability to change the way we look at maths.

Let me give you an insight on the use of this formula.

We have the equation n = n+1

Let n = 0

Then, 0=1 (1)

Now let n=1

Then, 1=2 (2)

Equating (1) and (2) we get 0 = 1 = 2

In the same way, if we keep repeating the process, you will see that this gives us the conclusion that all numbers are equal. This is something which sound truely impossible as how can 1 dollar and 10 dollars be equal? They have different values, but this equation shows us the proof that all of them are equal.

This is why I stated that this formula has the capability to change the way we look at Mathematics. It gives mathematics a new light.

# IX

# The Conclusion

After all the derivations and theories let me summarize them up here :

1) The series - (1+1+1+1+1+1+1+1...) converges to both 0 and 1

   2) The series - (1-1-1-1-1-1-1-1-1...) also converges to both 0 and 1

   3) The simplification of the 3 series - (1+1+1+1...) , (1-1-1-1...) and (1+2+3+4...) lead to the equation

   $0 = 1$

   4) All the theories after combining and the deduction of these points lead to the mathematically impossible

   equation : $n = n+1$

   5) All these theories lead to a point which tells us that all the numbers in existence are equal.

After having a look at these theories, you must be able to make out how far Mathematics still has to go.

   We still have loopholes in Mathematics and believe if these loopholes are solved, we might discover things which are completely unknown in today's time.

# X

# The Paradox

Now, as you have observed we have been able to prove things which were named as 'impossible'. But, what do we get after proving and deriving such equations?

You see, when I was able to prove this theory I started to develop new theories from the results I achieved. There maybe some theories, which are completely unbelievable, but after seeing this much I believe it is just a matter of time until something new will explode.

So, let me give you a brief on the theories which I have come up until now.

- So the first among them, after we have been able to prove that all numbers are equal, the main question arises is what is that specific constant which is equal to all these numbers? Because, think of it this way, if all numbers are equal, then what will they be equal to? We need some specific constant to which all the numbers are equal.

- The next question I have in mind is, if all numbers are equal then what really is infinity now? Because till now, we only thought about infinity as something never ending or unreachable, but now after these proofs, if we say that all numbers are equal, will infinity also be equal to that specific constant?

- Let me give you my theory on the creation of numbers. Now, lets imagine that the constant $\varphi$ is the number equal to all other numbers. Imagine $\varphi$ as a huge rock. Now, start breaking this rock into small pieces, the first one very small then the second one a bit larger than the first one, then the third one a little larger than the second one and so on...

- Keep in mind, the rock currently is so big that we can't even see the whole rock. We keep breaking part by part out of it. I believe this is what we call infinity. I believe Infinity is that number which has the ability to be equal to all other numbers. Because, currently as we believe, nothing is greater than infinity itself.

- So, to conclude this theory, I believe **Infinity is the start of all numbers and Infinity is the end of all numbers.**

# XI

# About the Future

In this section, I would like to talk about what I plan to do in the future regarding these theories and derivations. Currently, my main motive of publishing this book is so that I can keep a record of my derivations and also prove that I am the rightful creator of these theories.

As you must have already seen, this book is the $1^{st}$ volume of a series of books which I plan to publish.
Currently I have been working on some more theories and researching more about these theories. I will be recording those theories in the second volume of the book.

These theories, have been something I always thought about. But, I never had any proof to prove my points, but now I have the proofs, I have the derivation and I have all the theories listed in this very book.

So, I would like to thank you all for spending your time into reading this book. I will make sure to release some even more interesting theories in the future.

# XII
# About the Author

Here, I would like to tell you about myself and how I started to like Mathematics. From the beginning of my childhood I have always been focused on solving problems. It is because of that which I have good logical thinking skills.

My parents were the ones encouraging me to put all my efforts into my academics. Although they made sure to remind me to spend time on extracurricular activities. They made me learn how to play guitar, enrolled me in a football coaching for some time, bought me a chess board so I could practice playing chess and what not. I am the most grateful to them, because without them, I would be nothing today, absolutely nothing.

One more important person who helped me was my brother. He always picked competitions with me which motivated me to beat him. You know, it's the natural tendency between brothers to fight and that is what made the best out of me. I thank my brother for the same.

I have always had an edge towards problem solving, and I think that is why I started to love maths. Till class 7$^{th}$ or 8$^{th}$ I was still, a normal child who was a little good in academics.

But, the times turned when I was in 9$^{th}$. I had changed my school, and saw a lot more competitors than before. One of them, Hiten, was an expert in Physics, one of them named Tejaswa, was also a decent Mathematics student like me and one other named Akshita, who was my overall academic competitor.

Nonetheless, these were the sutdents, who motivated me to study harder and that was when I started putting extra efforts. I started to solve books of higher levels, I started studying the theory of class 10$^{th}$ and 11$^{th}$ and solving a lot more problems. They were the ones who changed me to this extent.

Currently, I am studying the basics for class 11$^{th}$ and 12$^{th}$, because in the future I plan to take the JEE exam. It is a good way to improve my knowledge and it also gives me a boost of motivation to study even more.

So, if you want to know what things I have specifically done to come up to here, the answer is hard work. I have solved a lot of questions related to the same topic again and again. I have some people who say to me that I have been god-gifted and that is why I am so smart, but even if you are born god-gifted, it is of no use if you don't know how to increase your potential. We all have a lot of potential in ourselves and if you put your hard work into it, you can also be equivalent to the 'god gifted' people.

I myself, used to solve 200-300 questions a day when I was in 9th. All I could see were question at that time. Of course, I used to have problems in specific topics too, but that didn't mean I could give up and pick up something else. If that would be my attitude, I would be no more than a failure.

# XIII

## About the Book

The book "**The Magic Behind Numbers**" is a book, which explains the findings and theories developed by a 14 year old student. This book focuses on bending mathematics to shape it to how you want. Because, Mathematics is not a rigid subject, rather it is flexible.

What I mean by that is, Mathematics can be changed from time to time to solve new problems and come up with interesting theories. One such example of the same is the topic "imaginary numbers" and the concept of iota. A simple equation $x^2+1 = 0$ could not be solved, until we had to introduce iota - that is the square root of (-1).

So, this book focuses on the bending of mathematics to create some interesting theories which have the ability to change the course of mathematics.

I hope you must have enjoyed this book, I plan to release the second volume of this book after all the research has been done for it.

Thank you!